The 100
Most Entertaining Predictions
About the 21st Century

(The Wacky, the Weird, and the Wise)

By William and Lynette Ray

The 100 Most Entertaining Predictions

About the 21st Century

Copyright © 2000 by William Ray.

ISBN-13: 978-1720794615

ISBN-10: 1720794618

Seaborne Books

DEDICATION

In loving memories of our fathers,

Floyd J. Ray and Robert E. Tuggle

ACKNOWLEDGEMENTS

We'd like to thank Shauna and Larry Catania for their encouragement and help from start to finish.

CONTENTS

INTRODUCTION

For centuries, the turning of the 21st century has attracted predictions like a windshield attracts bugs. "Prophets," predictors, and prognosticators have felt compelled to tell us what was going to happen at the dawn of the third millennium.

Now that we're there, we thought it would be fun to research what has been predicted about our day and see how the predictions turned out. The result is *The 100 Most Entertaining Predictions About the 21st Century.*

Some of the predictions are wacky (see Underwear Converted into Candy). Some are surprisingly accurate (see Modern Gas Stations). On some the jury is still out: Will "hovercraft" replace the automobile? (see Highways Give Way to Hovercraft).

The predictions come from all sorts: psychics, "seers," modern scientists, sci-fi writers, inventors, futurists, religious leaders, astrologers—even future prime ministers. And they come from centuries past— the earliest from the Great Pyramid at Giza, built around 2700 B.C. (see So Says the Pyramid)—down to modern times.

There was a multitude of predictions to choose from—predictions gathered from rare books no longer in print (that had to be shipped to us across the nation), from crumbling magazine collections a hundred years old, from the weird ravings of modern psychics, from the supermarket tabloids, from the pages of *Time* and *Newsweek*.

We narrowed the horde down to the 100 we found the most interesting. We hope you enjoy them as much as we did.

"Do not be afraid. I am the First and the Last."

-        Revelation 1:17

THE 100TH MOST ENTERTAINING PREDICTION

You Won't Look a Day Over 40

Waldemar Kaempffert, Science Editor of the *New York Times*, predicted that senior citizens in the 21st century would not look a day over 40.

In his 1950 *Popular Mechanics* article, entitled "Miracles You'll See In The Next Fifty Years," Kaempffert said increased knowledge of metabolism and hormones would enable doctors "to treat old age as a degenerative disease. Men and women of 70 in A.D. 2000 look as if they were 40. Wrinkles, sagging cheeks, leathery skins are curiosities or signs of neglect."

THE 99TH MOST ENTERTAINING PREDICTION

So Says the Pyramid

The Great Pyramid at Giza, built around 2700 B.C., predicted the world would end on September 17, 2001.

This from a theory first put forth by Charles Piazzi Smyth, a nineteenth century royal astronomer in Scotland. According to the theory, the inside passageways of the pyramid foretell the major events of history. Each rough inch or so, starting at the original entrance, represents a year. Big events like the flood and the birth of Christ are marked by niches and corners in the walls.

Why would the world end on September 17, 2001? That's when the passageways run out of inches.

THE 98TH MOST ENTERTAINING PREDICTION

Jumping Out the Office Window

Futurist Buckminster Fuller predicted modern man, at the end of a day, would jump out the office window and fly home.

In a 1968 *McCall's*, he imagined that in "the next twenty years" we would "strap on our jet-stilts knapsack, jump Peter Pan-wise to our office window ledge ... and wing outward and homeward by automatically steered, collision-avoiding beam controls."

THE 97TH MOST ENTERTAINING PREDICTION

$30 Trillion in Frozen Bodies

According to a 1967 *New York Times Magazine* article, entitled "They Live In The Year 2000," science fiction writer Frederik Pohl predicted a "$30 trillion" market in cryonics—the business of freezing people facing death until a remedy is found for their ailment.

Pohl was speaking to a convention of life insurance agents in Chicago. He told them they had expanded their "market as far as possible through selling pension plans, annuities and the like," and should begin to concentrate on cryonics, the "$30-trillion market of the future." How would insurance companies prosper from cryonics? By "writing policies to cover the storage cost" of the frozen bodies.

Medical Experiments on Felons

Novelist Samuel Madden envisioned medical experiments on felons by the 21st century.

In his 1733 novel, *Memoirs of the Twentieth Century* —one of the first futuristic novels ever—"the lives and bodies of ... condemn'd Felons" are given to medical researchers "to try all such experiments on, which they judg'd useful to improve their Science." This saved the lives of many "honest" people by "substituting Malefactors to be purg'd, blooded, and vomited" in their place.

THE 95TH MOST ENTERTAINING PREDICTION

Popes Harmed

In her 1969 book, *Jeane Dixon, My Life and Prophecies*, the psychic predicted: "During this century one pope will suffer bodily harm. Another will be assassinated."

A terrorist shot and wounded Pope John Paul II outside St. Peter's Basilica in May 1981. He recovered and as of this writing continues his duties.

German Empire

Henry Paradyne predicted a German empire would "straddle Europe" by 2009.

In a 1909 *Harper's Weekly* article, entitled "The World in 2009," Paradyne also said: "The twentieth century will be inevitably Germany's—and never has any nation so thoroughly deserved that triumph and success which she has now to reap."

THE 93RD MOST ENTERTAINING PREDICTION

Ireland Relocated

Winston Churchill predicted the utilization of nuclear power.

In a 1932 *Popular Mechanics* article, entitled "Fifty Years Hence," the future prime minister predicted: "Geography and climate would obey our orders" with this new source of energy, and he cited some far-out possibilities—shifting "Ireland into the middle of the Atlantic," thawing "all the ice at the arctic and antarctic poles."

Nuclear science pioneers had made advances before Churchill's prediction, but no practical use of their knowledge was found until 1938 when the process of nuclear fission was discovered.

THE 92ND MOST ENTERTAINING PREDICTION

Lasting Peace in 2002?

Nostradamus predicted lasting world peace would begin sometime around the year 2002, according to one of his many interpreters, Dr. Christian Wollner (*The Mystery of Nostradamus*, 1926).

Nostradamus wrote:

"Mars and the sceptre will be in conjunction,

"Under Cancer, a calamitous war:

"A little while after there will be a new king anointed

"Who for a long time shall pacify the earth."

-*Centuries*, 6.24

Wollner said this Mars under Cancer conjunction takes place on June 21, 2002.

THE 91ST MOST ENTERTAINING PREDICTION

Earth Knocked Off its Orbit

A psychic named Criswell predicted the world would end before the 21st century—in fact, on August 18, 1999.

How? A magnetic disturbance will deprive the Earth of its oxygen. The Earth will be knocked off its orbit and race toward the sun. Humans on 200 space stations will be left to themselves.

THE 90TH MOST ENTERTAINING PREDICTION

China Invades the Middle East

Psychic Jeane Dixon predicted China would invade the Middle East around the year 2000.

In her 1969 book, Jeane Dixon, My Life and Prophecies , she said: "I have projected my quest for information into the year 2000 and see Chinese and Mongol troops invading the Middle East."

THE 89TH MOST ENTERTAINING PREDICTION

Freight Shipped Cross-Country by Air Tube

Robert O'Brien talked about the possibility that freight would be shipped across the country through air-powered pipelines.

In his 1962 *Reader's Digest* article, entitled "Forty Years From Now," O'Brien wrote: "Trucks may be museum pieces; supplies and freight may cross the nation through pneumatic pipelines, with electronic sensing devices to guide shipments through the system to their destination."

Ship of Pearls

Psychic Bertie Catchings predicted there would be a startling discovery in California in 1996: "In a desert area of southern California, a ship will be unearthed that holds a great store of pearls."

THE 87TH MOST ENTERTAINING PREDICTION

"Aerocar" Garage

In the late 1920's architect R.A. Duncan unveiled his house of the year 2000 in a full size exhibit in London. He predicted the home would have need of an "aerocar" garage to house the family's "combination airplane-automobile," which would have "folding wings" and a movable propeller that could be adjusted for airplane-style flight or positioned above the car "for straight ascent as a helicopter."

THE 86TH MOST ENTERTAINING PREDICTION

33

Highways Give Way to Hovercraft

A 1966 *Time* article, citing Marshall McLuhan and other futurists, predicted the present day automobile would be replaced by "hovercraft" by the year 2000.

Said the article: "... both the wheel and the highway will be obsolete, giving way to hovercraft that ride on air."

THE 85TH MOST ENTERTAINING PREDICTION

All-Wheel Steering

If the following prediction by the editors of the *Kiplinger Letters* comes true, parallel parking in the 21st century will be a breeze: cars, they said, will "have all-wheel steering, so you can maneuver more nimbly in traffic and sideslip easily into tight parking spaces."

THE 84TH MOST ENTERTAINING PREDICTION

The Life Span of Cars

In 1987 the World Future Society predicted the life span of the average year 2000 car would be 22 years—compared to 7.5 at the time of the prediction.

Check your garage.

THE 83RD MOST ENTERTAINING PREDICTION

Good-bye to Black Ink on White Pages

In David Goodman Croly's 1888 book, *Glimpses of the Future: Suggestions as to the Drift of Things —* which he said was "To be read now and judged in the year 2000"—a character named Mr. Fanciful laments the dull tradition of black ink on white pages, color scheme he believes destroys vision. He says, "I predict that the literature of the future will be printed in the colors of nature ... greens, blues, and other hues grateful to the human eye. If we ever have a permanent literature, it will probably be a yellow ink on a background of dark blue."

THE 82ND MOST ENTERTAINING PREDICTION

Moral Breakdown

H.G. Wells (*The Time Machine*, *The War of the Worlds*) predicted moral breakdown in modern society.

In his 1901 *North American Review* series, about "the way things will probably go in this new century," he predicted marital unions "of every variable status," and that "vice and depravity, in every form that is not absolutely penal ... practised in every grade of magnificence and condoned." And he gave his reasons: "religion will no longer speak with a unanimous voice," a mobile population ("freedom of escape from disapproving neighbors"), the proliferation of the idly prosperous, and the media.

THE 81ST MOST ENTERTAINING PREDICTION

Abortion

R. G. Ruste, in his 1967 book *American Heritage Prognosis A.D. 2000*, predicted the legalization of abortion: "Because no method of birth control seems to function with 100% success, it follows that abortion must become legally and socially acceptable. By the year A.D. 2000, no female will be under the slightest compulsion to bear a child under any circumstances. The law and the mores will by then recognize that whether to bear a child or not is entirely a matter of choice by the female concerned."

The Supreme Court legalized abortion in the U.S. in 1973 in the Roe v. Wade decision.

THE 80TH MOST ENTERTAINING PREDICTION

Women's Work?

R.G. Ruste predicted women would excel in medicine and law, but stay away from any work that "breaks the fingernails."

In his 1967 book, *American Heritage Prognosis A.D. 2000*, Ruste said: "Women will take possession of the field of medicine, even as they now do in Russia. Law will also be dominated by women—Work that mars personal daintiness will remain men's work. Women will not engage in mechanical repair work or anything else that stains the hands, breaks the fingernails, lessens personal attractiveness in any way."

THE 79TH MOST ENTERTAINING PREDICTION

A Woman President

Psychic Jeane Dixon predicted a female president before the 21st century.

In her 1969 book, *Jeane Dixon, My Life and Prophecies*, she predicted a female president "in the not too distant future—timing is difficult to get, but I feel it will surely be in the 1980's."

THE 78TH MOST ENTERTAINING PREDICTION

Freeways Converted into Skating Rinks

Futurist Buckminster Fuller, a 1966 lecture at San Jose State College in California, predicted the American highway was on its way out: "We get onto a freeway … running in lines in opposite directions at 65 miles an hour, only five feet apart, with everybody practicing steering. A decade from now this will look rather silly … we will finish with our great highway programs just in time to turn them into some kind of roller-skating rink."

No More Ironing

A Westinghouse Electric Corporation scientist predicted an end to the chore of ironing.

In a 1967 *U.S. News & World Report* article, Dr. W.E. Shoupp said: "Ironing in the year 2000 will be a thing of the past. All clothing will be made from fabrics that come with permanent creases ... Even the bums in the park will look like Beau Brummel."

THE 76TH MOST ENTERTAINING PREDICTION

A Tunnel to America

The book *Golf in the Year 2000*, published in London in 1892, imagined a tunnel from London to New York in the year 2000—this trip under the Atlantic Ocean, by means of the "Transatlantic Tubular Railway," would take only 2 hours and 32 minutes.

THE 75TH MOST ENTERTAINING PREDICTION

Bridges Across the Atlantic

According to the 1980 book *The People's Almanac Presents The Book of Predictions*, psychic Bertie Catchings predicted "flexible bridges" would stretch across the Atlantic Ocean by the 21st century: "You will be able to walk across the Atlantic Ocean. There will be many cities on this ocean, linked by flexible bridges."

THE 74TH MOST ENTERTAINING PREDICTION

"A Milk Faucet in Every Kitchen!"

Secretary of Agriculture Orville L. Freeman predicted that milk would be piped to homes just like water.

A 1968 *McCall's* article, entitled "Menu for the Year 2000," reported: "Secretary of Agriculture Orville L. Freeman would not be at all surprised if, at some time in the future, [milk] went directly from processing plants to the consumers in sanitized pipelines. A milk faucet in every kitchen!"

THE 73RD MOST ENTERTAINING PREDICTION

Growing Chicken Parts

Winston Churchill predicted chicken wings and breasts, etc., would be grown for consumption separately—without the need of raising a whole chicken.

In a 1932 *Popular Mechanics* article, entitled "Fifty Years Hence," the future prime minister wrote: "With a greater knowledge of what are called hormones, i.e., the chemical messengers in our blood, it will be possible to control growth. We shall escape the absurdity of growing a whole chicken in order to eat the breast or wing, by growing these parts separately under a suitable medium."

THE 72ND MOST ENTERTAINING PREDICTION

Man Will Fly (from Hill to Hill)

David Goodman Croly predicted man was on the eve of flight 15 years before the Wright brothers' success, but he imagined some interesting consequences.

In his 1888 book, *Glimpses of the Future: Suggestions as to the Drift of Things*—which he said was "To be read now and judged in the year 2000"—he said it would cost "thousands of lives" to bring about the invention of flight, and that it would have an odd impact on population distribution: "As it is easier to fly from hill-top to hill-top than from valley to valley, the latter will lose in population, and the former gain." He also said: "I do not see how heavy freight can ever be carried through the atmosphere."

THE 71ST MOST ENTERTAINING PREDICTION

Oprah Buys CBS

"Seer" Luna Diamond predicted in the December 16, 1997, issue of the *National Examiner* that Oprah Winfrey would buy CBS in 1998 and dedicate it "to wholesome family viewing, making it the first major network to turn its back on TV violence."

THE 70TH MOST ENTERTAINING PREDICTION

Sharon Stone Rescues Plane from Hijacker

The December 16, 1997, issue of the *National Examiner* also cited a prediction by Chicago psychic "Christy" that in 1998 actress Sharon Stone would help "foil an airline disaster when she talks a suicidal hijacker out of his deadly plan."

THE 69TH MOST ENTERTAINING PREDICTION

Paid to be Idle

A 1966 *Time* article predicted that, due to replacement by computers, "only 10% of the population will be working, and the rest will, in effect, have to be paid to be idle."

The article, entitled "The Futurists: Looking Toward A.D. 2000," quoted John Fisher of Tempo (Technical Management Planning Organization): "By 1984, man will spend the first third of his life, or 25 years, getting an education, only the second one-third working, and the final third enjoying the fruits of his labor. There just won't be enough work to go around. Moonlighting will become as socially unacceptable as bigamy."

THE 68TH MOST ENTERTAINING PREDICTION

Earth Admitted to Interstellar Federation

In 1980 psychic Francie Steiger predicted that "Earth would be admitted to the Interstellar Federation" in 2001. "We will receive the aliens' assistance in developing new technologies and mental abilities, ushering in a Golden Age for humanity."

THE 67TH MOST ENTERTAINING PREDICTION

Mechanical Doctors

Walter Cronkite looked forward to the possibility of receiving a medical exam just by sitting in a chair.

In a 1967 article for *Popular Science Monthly*, entitled "The Twenty-First Century: The World You'll Live In" —billed by the magazine as "a startling glimpse into the year 2000 and beyond"—Cronkite wrote about some of the futuristic hardware he had tested in research for his television series The 21st Century. For example: "Another feature medicine will offer in years to come is a 'mechanical doctor'—like Philco's medical monitoring chair. It looks like an ordinary office chair. I sat in it fully clothed with my hands on the arms. I felt no sensation. A slight bulge at the back held a microphone. I was told there were concealed sensors in the arms. In a few seconds, the doctor showed me my examination results: a complete electrocardiogram as well as other tests, neatly printed on graph paper."

Square Tomatoes

Standard Oil suggested square tomatoes were in our future.

As part of its display at the 1962 Seattle World's Fair, Standard Oil of California predicted that the farm of the 21st century might "grow fruits and vegetables in arbitrary shapes that package well—for instance, square tomatoes."

THE 65TH MOST ENTERTAINING PREDICTION

A Paradise for Womankind

Novelist Edward Bellamy predicted there would be no housework in the year 2000.

In his 1887 novel, *Looking Backward, 2000-1887,* a citizen of the nineteenth century falls into a hypnotic sleep and wakes up in year 2000 Boston. When he asks who is in charge of the housework, his hostess replies, "There is none to do ... Our washing is all done at public laundries at excessively cheap rates, and our cooking at public kitchens. The making and repairing of all we wear are done outside in public shops. Electricity ... takes the place of all fires and lighting. We choose houses no larger than we need, and furnish them so as to involve the minimum of trouble to keep them in order." Upon hearing these words, the citizen of the nineteenth century exclaims, "What a paradise for womankind the world must be now!"

THE 64TH MOST ENTERTAINING PREDICTION

Hot Walls

H.G. Wells (*The Time Machine, The War of the Worlds*) imagined that air conditioning would turn out a little differently than it did..

In a 1901 *North American Review* article about "the way things will probably go in this new century," Wells predicted: "The house of the future will probably be warmed in its walls from some power-generating station ... air will enter the house of the future through proper tubes in the walls, which will warm it and capture its dust, and it will be spun out again by a simple mechanism."

THE 63RD MOST ENTERTAINING PREDICTION

Air Conditioning Faucets

John Elfreth Watkins, Jr., foresaw today's air-conditioned home—sort of.

In a 1900 *Ladies' Home Journal* article, entitled "What May Happen In The Next Hundred Years," Watkins said: "Hot or cold air will be turned on from spigots to regulate the temperature of a house as we now turn on hot or cold water from spigots to regulate the temperature of the bath ... Rising early to build the furnace fire will be a task of the olden times."

Willis Carrier designed the first mechanical air conditioner in 1911.

THE 62ND MOST ENTERTAINING PREDICTION

A Thermostat in Your Clothes

A 1962 *Science News Letter* article predicted that clothes in the year 2000 would come with temperature controls.

The article, "Happy Home Life, Year 2000," said clothing "will feature lapel dials that can be adjusted to increase or decrease the output of thermoelectric temperature controls built into the garments."

THE 61ˢᵀ MOST ENTERTAINING PREDICTION

Hosing Down the Living Room

Waldemar Kaempffert, Science Editor of the *New York Times*, predicted the housewife of the year 2000 would simply hose down her living room to clean it.

In his 1950 *Popular Mechanics* article, entitled "Miracles You'll See In The Next Fifty Years," Kaempffert said: "Why not? Furniture (upholstery included), rugs, draperies, unscratchable floors—all are made of synthetic fabric or waterproof plastic. After the water has run down a drain in the middle of the floor (later concealed by a rug of synthetic fiber) Jane turns on a blast of hot air and dries everything. A detergent in the water dissolves any resistant dirt."

THE 60TH MOST ENTERTAINING PREDICTION

No Tolerance for the Nonproductive

David Goodman Croly predicted there would be no tolerance for the nonproductive in the society of the future.

In his 1888 book, *Glimpses of the Future: Suggestions as to the Drift of Things*—which he said was "To be read now and judged in the year 2000"— Croly said: "In the coming scientific age there will be less sentimentalism than there is now. Men and women will not be allowed to drink themselves to death. The tramp will not be tolerated ... the law will go so far as to prevent the criminal and diseased from marrying and having families. Children will not be born under conditions that will ensure them life-long misery—or make them a peril to the community."

THE 59TH MOST ENTERTAINING PREDICTION

Household Robots

A *Time* article predicted very helpful "household robots" by the 21st century.

The 1966 article, entitled "The Futurists: Looking Toward A.D. 2000," predicted robots "would wash dishes, dispose of the garbage (onto a conveyer belt moving under the street), vacuum rugs, wash windows, cut the grass," and "play a mean game of pingpong."

No Smoking

Paul Devinne predicted an end to smoking.

In his 1902 futuristic novel, *The Day of Prosperity*, a citizen of the year 2000 says: "Why, no one uses tobacco now. It is generations since any one has smoked." Another citizen of 2000 explains how this happened: "The women were opposed to it, and by degrees it was forbidden."

THE 57TH MOST ENTERTAINING PREDICTION

Municipal Umbrella

Novelist Edward Bellamy predicted that by the 21st century a huge umbrella would be rolled out over the city whenever it rained.

He made the prediction in his 1887 novel *Looking Backward, 2000-1887*, which is set in the year 2000, where it is "considered an extraordinary imbecility to permit the weather to have any effect on the social movements of the people." Instead "a continuous waterproof covering" is rolled out over sidewalks and intersections when it rains, so that whereas "in the nineteenth century, when it rained, the people of Boston put up three hundred thousand umbrellas over as many heads ... in the twentieth century they put up one umbrella over all the heads."

THE 56TH MOST ENTERTAINING PREDICTION

World Population

The Stanford Research Institute, in a 1959 study for the Senate Foreign Relations Committee, predicted that by the year 2000 world population would be "a total of 6,267,000,000 people."

As of 1995, world population was about 5,813,000,000. It was increasing at an annual rate of 1.6 percent, which would put world population in the year 2000 at about 6.3 billion—right on target with the Stanford Research Institute's forecast.

By the way, world population in 1650 was 550 million. It took 200 years (until 1850) for that figure to double. Since then population has increased nearly five times.

THE 55TH MOST ENTERTAINING PREDICTION

No More Racial Prejudice

In 1962 Martin Luther King, Jr., predicted there would be an end to prejudice.

He actually said it would happen by 1987: the world would "blush with shame to recall that, three decades earlier, a human being was graded by the color of his skin and degraded if that color was not white. I would expect the Christian era to begin."

THE 54TH MOST ENTERTAINING PREDICTION

End of the Cold War

David Ben-Gurion, Prime Minister of Israel, foresaw the end of the Cold War.

In a 1962 *Look*, he said that by 1987 the Cold War would "be a thing of the past." He missed it by only a few years: the Soviet Union, under internal economic and political pressure, dissolved into a number of independent states in 1991.

THE 53RD MOST ENTERTAINING PREDICTION

Boswash, Chipitts, and Sansan

Futurist Herman Kahn predicted sprawling megalopolises would embrace half the American population.

In the 1974 Hudson Institute report, *A Slightly Optimistic World Context for 1975-2000*, he said the three largest megalopolises would be Boswash (an urban sprawl that would swallow every city between Boston and Washington), Chipitts (joining Chicago and Pittsburgh and the cities in between), and Sansan (stretching from San Diego to San Francisco).

THE 52ND MOST ENTERTAINING PREDICTION

Cure for the Cold

A 1962 *Reader's Digest* article predicted, "By 2002 … victory over the common cold and other upper respiratory infections will be medical history."

The article gushed on, "It seems probable that a single injection, or pill, will immunize us against all communicable ailments."

And: "Specialists may be able to determine our susceptibility to cancer, and, if necessary, ward it off with anti-cancer vaccines."

THE 51ST MOST ENTERTAINING PREDICTION

A Really Easy Pregnancy

A 1966 *Time* article, entitled "The Futurists: Looking Toward A.D. 2000," looked forward to a really easy pregnancy for women: "Medical men foresee fetuses grown outside the uterus (in case women want to be spared the burdens of pregnancy)..."

THE 50TH MOST ENTERTAINING PREDICTION

Canada Claimed by the U.S.

David Goodman Croly predicted the U.S. would annex Canada, and not necessarily peacefully.

In his 1888 book, *Glimpses of the Future: Suggestions as to the Drift of Things*—which he said was "To be read now and judged in the year 2000"— he said there was "every human reason why this dependency of Great Britain should become a part of our Union, but the unnatural barriers in the way will probably finally be broken down by force."

THE 49TH MOST ENTERTAINING PREDICTION

Specialized Breeding of Humans

Winston Churchill predicted that before the 21st century science would have the ability to breed some human beings for mental work and others for physical work.

In a 1932 *Popular Mechanics* article, entitled "Fifty Years Hence," the future prime minister of Great Britain said: "There seems little doubt that it will be possible to carry out the entire cycle which now leads to the birth of a child, in artificial surroundings. Interference with the mental development of such beings, expert suggestion and treatment in the earlier years, would produce beings specialized to thought or toil."

THE 48TH MOST ENTERTAINING PREDICTION

Modern Gas Stations

The editors of the *Kiplinger Letters*, in their 1986 book, foresaw the gas station of today: "Say goodbye to the old-fashioned gas station with the repair shop in back. The service station of the 2000s will be neat, even antiseptic, looking something like a credit bureau with gas pumps out front ... Most of the bigger ones will be highly automated 24-hour operations, equipped with pumps that accept credit or debit cards and print out a receipt."

THE 47TH MOST ENTERTAINING PREDICTION

Women Make No Bad Marriages

Women in the 21st century will make no bad marriages.

According to Edward Bellamy's 1887 utopian novel, *Looking Backward, 2000-1887* (a best-seller in its day, only *Uncle Tom's Cabin* printing as many copies in its first two years), any woman of the year 2000 who considers marriage to an unproductive man faces the censure "of her own sex." Women will teach "their daughters from childhood" to mate selectively to ensure progress for the human race from generation to generation.

THE 46TH MOST ENTERTAINING PREDICTION

Fashions Never Change

Paul Devinne predicted women in the year 2000 would be unconcerned about their appearance and as a result fashions would remain constant.

In his 1902 novel, *The Day of Prosperity*, a lady of the year 2000 explains to a visitor from the early 1900s that "the present style is about fifty years old, and I see no signs of change." Another lady adds, "We outgrew all that ages ago. You know, women give hardly a thought to their external appearance now."

THE 45TH MOST ENTERTAINING PREDICTION

Distant Events Relayed By Mirrors

The book *Golf in the Year 2000* predicted that distant events would be relayed to private homes by means of mirrors.

In the book, which was published in London in 1892, a citizen of 1892 falls into a trance and awakens in the year 2000. A London play, he discovers, is relayed by means of mirrors to a private home, where it is viewed live on another mirror, the sound being provided over the telephone. Giant mirrors are also suspended over golf courses to reflect important matches to viewers in distant places.

THE 44TH MOST ENTERTAINING PREDICTION

State-of-the-Art Home for $5000

Waldemar Kaempffert, Science Editor for the *New York Times*, predicted that the home of the year 2000—with "all its furnishings ... galeproof and weatherproof"—would cost $5000.

He made his prediction in a 1950 *Popular Mechanics* article, entitled "Miracles You'll See In The Next Fifty Years." However, the median sales price for a new home in 1996 was $140,000, according to the U.S. Bureau of the Census.

THE 43RD MOST ENTERTAINING PREDICTION

Domed Cities

In a 1968 *McCall's* that focused on the "beginning of the third millennium," futurist Buckminster Fuller predicted domed cities: "Cities will roof their centers over with vast translucent domes, enabling mass air conditioning and weatherproofing. One dome could cover Manhattan from river to river and from 22nd Street to 62nd Street, rising about three quarters of a mile over the Empire State Building and containing less steel than the Queen Mary."

Talking Plants

So you think it strange some people talk to their plants? California psychic Sandra McNeil predicted that by 1990 the plants would talk back.

According to the 1980 book Predictions, McNeil said this would come about by means of a computer analyzer that would convert a plant's vibrations into a human voice.

THE 41ST MOST ENTERTAINING PREDICTION

The Speed of Light

In 1733, novelist Samuel Madden ventured a guess at the speed of light. In his novel, *Memoirs of the Twentieth Century*, one of the first futuristic novels ever written, he predicted that by the end of the twentieth century man would have discovered the speed of light to be "500,000 miles in a minute."

The speed of light is 186,282 miles per second.

THE 40TH MOST ENTERTAINING PREDICTION

Basketball Goals 12 Feet High

Sportswriter Martin Abramson predicted that by 1989 basketball goals would be raised from 10 feet to 12 feet high to win back fans tired of seeing "teams composed of giants who can amass large scores by stuffing balls in the basket instead of shooting."

Goals are still ten feet high, the "dunk" gets the loudest cheers, and the NBA has skyrocketed in popularity since Abramson's prediction in 1980.

THE 39TH MOST ENTERTAINING PREDICTION

Earthscrapers

In 1980 psychic counselor and hypnotist Ann Fisher predicted that by the year 2000 we would "witness an underground revolution, with skyscraper-type buildings placed deep in the earth and sealed against water."

THE 38TH MOST ENTERTAINING PREDICTION

Moats Come Back in Style

Psychic counselor and hypnotist Ann Fisher also predicted that by 1989 there would "be a revival of moats like those around medieval castles. They will be used to provide security for new government buildings and for the homes of the wealthy."

THE 37TH MOST ENTERTAINING PREDICTION

Marriage for Family, Marriage for Pleasure

In a 1968 *McCall's* article, Patricia R. Harris forecast the possibility of a new 21st century custom, that of each individual enjoying two marriages. "The first marriage," she said, "will be for the purpose of founding a family ... The second marriage will be for the purpose of personal and sexual fulfillment."

THE 36TH MOST ENTERTAINING PREDICTION

Sex for Efficiency Only

H.G. Wells (*The Time Machine*, *The War of the Worlds*) predicted that sex would be for efficiency only.

In his 1901 *The North American Review* series, about "the way things will probably go in this new century," he said sex for the productive and inventive person of the twentieth century would be "without any trappings of sentiment and mysticism," and would be treated only as "a concession to the flesh necessary to secure efficiency."

Ice Age

Chicago "parascientist" Irene Hughes predicted in 1980 that an ice age would be fully upon us by 1989. (As I write this line, it's about 100 degrees outside my window here in the Arizona desert.)

THE 34TH MOST ENTERTAINING PREDICTION

California Earthquake

Tobacco Road author Erskine Caldwell, perhaps tongue-in-cheek, predicted that in the year 2000 "California from San Francisco to Los Angeles will at last become the victim of an earthquake and disappear into a black hole while being televised by ABC, NBC, CBS, and PBS."

THE 33RD MOST ENTERTAINING PREDICTION

Rats, the Plague, and Celebrities

In the December 16, 1997, issue of the *National Examiner*, "seer" Luna Diamond predicted that in 1998 "Rats carrying the deadly bubonic plague" would "overrun Los Angeles, sparking mass evacuations. Panic erupts among celebrities as they desperately hunt for homes in plague-free zones like Idaho, Colorado and New York state."

THE 32ND MOST ENTERTAINING PREDICTION

Rockin' Royals, Regis Philbin, & Roseanne

The December 16, 1997, issue of the *National Examiner* published a prediction by 12-year-old "seer" Miranda Sloan. Miss Sloan predicted that in 1998 Prince William would display "a hidden singing talent" and start the chart-topping band "The Rockin' Royals"—with profits to "go to Princess Di's charitable foundations."

Miss Sloan also predicted that Regis Philbin would get "fed up with showbiz shenanigans" and head off "to medical school."

And Roseanne would "disappear for six weeks, setting off massive searches by police departments all over America. She will be found wandering the streets in Fargo, N.D., where she'll tell authorities she was abducted by space aliens."

THE 31ST MOST ENTERTAINING PREDICTION

Alien Virus

Science fiction writer Philip K. Dick speculated that in the year 2000 "An alien virus, brought back by an interplanetary ship, will decimate the population of Earth ..."

THE 30TH MOST ENTERTAINING PREDICTION

Men on Mars

A 1966 *Time* article cited a Rand Corporation study in which "82 scientists agreed that a permanent lunar base will have been established long before A.D. 2000 and that men will have flown past Venus and landed on Mars."

THE 29TH MOST ENTERTAINING PREDICTION

Commuters through Tunnels at 500 mph

A 1962 *Science News Letter* article, entitled "Happy Home Life, Year 2000," predicted that between the year 2000 and the year 2050 "Commuters will be whisked through giant tunnels at speeds up to 500 miles per hour in cylinder-shaped vehicles driven by electromagnetism."

THE 28TH MOST ENTERTAINING PREDICTION

Family Helicopter Parked on the Roof

Waldemar Kaempffert, Science Editor of the *New York Times*, predicted helicopters would adorn the rooftops of homes in the 21st century neighborhood.

In a 1950 *Popular Mechanics* article, entitled "Miracles You'll See In The Next Fifty Years," Kaempffert predicted that for trips of "more than 20 miles" people of the year 2000 would "use the family helicopter, which is kept on the roof."

THE 27TH MOST ENTERTAINING PREDICTION

The American Highway of the Year 2000

Standard Oil of California, in a display at the 1962 Seattle World's Fair, pictured a pretty amazing American highway in the year 2000:

-Vehicles whisk "along on cushions of air" over electronically controlled lanes. "When a driver reaches his exit, he lets down the car's retractable wheels and drives off onto a noncontrolled access road."

-The roads "are surfaced with colored plastic, various hues indicating the fast, slow, and exit lanes."

-The roads are constructed by "machines that lay eight lanes of plastic pavement at the rate of five miles an hour. Sixty minutes later, the road is firm enough for traffic."

What's harder to believe: riding on cushions of air, or rapid road construction?

THE 26TH MOST ENTERTAINING PREDICTION

The White House in Minneapolis?

Tobacco Road author Erskine Caldwell, perhaps tongue-in-cheek, predicted the U.S. capital would move to Minneapolis in 1999.

According to the book *The People's Almanac Presents The Book of Predictions*, Caldwell (who died in 1987) said: "The U.S. government, including the Capitol, White House, taxis, spies, and call girls, will be moved and established in Minneapolis, Minn."

THE 25TH MOST ENTERTAINING PREDICTION

The Debit Card

The editors of the *Kiplinger Letters* predicted the popularity of the debit card.

In their 1986 book, *Kiplinger Forecasts: The New American Boom*, they predicted a cashless and checkless society would "be close at hand by the year 2000. Pocket money will probably consist of credit/debit cards plus a few coins and bills for the sake of habit, street vendors and small children. Paper checks will be available for personal use, but many or most businesses will not accept them—even from people with the best of credentials—or will charge a fee for accepting them."

THE 24TH MOST ENTERTAINING PREDICTION

Marlboro, Winston, and Marijuana

Shelley Levitt, editor of *High Times* and delegate to the International Cannabis Alliance for Reform, predicted the U.S. would legalize marijuana in 1997 "to bolster a worsening economy."

According to the book *The People's Almanac Presents The Book of Predictions*, Levitt predicted: "On the shelves of tobacco and liquor shops and in cigarette machines, one can purchase such brands as Connoisseur Colombian, Santa Marta Gold, Primo Mexican, and California Sinsemilla."

Levitt also predicted the U.S. would legalize cocaine: "It is sold in beautiful snuffboxes in liquor shops under names such as Peruvian Flake and Bolivian Rock."

THE 23RD MOST ENTERTAINING PREDICTION

Castro

Psychic Jeane Dixon expected Fidel Castro's rule to have ended long ago.

In her 1969 book, *Jeane Dixon, My Life and Prophecies*, she predicted: "Cuba's dictator, Fidel Castro, is rapidly losing both influence and power in his island government. On each occasion that I concentrate on him I see that his days in power are numbered because he is no longer useful to his Communist bosses ... I sense that he feels sudden death lurking around the corner and that it will not be a natural one."

Castro came to power in 1959, and is still there as of this writing.

Saddam Hussein's Rule Ends

Astrologer Noel Tyl predicted it was an "extremely low" probability that Saddam Hussein would be in power past July 1997.

In his 1996 book, *Predictions For A New Millennium*, he said: "A major astrological vector affects the horoscope for Iraq incontrovertibly. It is a signal of government overthrow; the party (person) in power is toppled, brought down."

THE 21ST MOST ENTERTAINING PREDICTION

No Man on the Moon

Waldemar Kaempffert, Science Editor of the *New York Times*, predicted man would not have traveled to the moon by the 21st century.

In a 1950 *Popular Mechanics* article, entitled "Miracles You'll See In The Next Fifty Years," Kaempffert said of the year 2000: "Nobody has yet circumnavigated the moon in a rocket space ship, but the idea is not laughed down."

THE 20TH MOST ENTERTAINING PREDICTION

Tragedy for the Royal Family

Astrologer Noel Tyl predicted "personal tragedy" for Prince Charles and his sons "in the Spring of 1997." In his 1996 book, *Predictions For A New Millennium*, Tyl said the tragedy would perhaps be "a death in the family that jars everyone."

Tyl was not far off. Princess Diana, Charles' ex-wife and the mother of his sons, was killed in the summer of 1997 in a high-speed car accident in Paris.

THE 19TH MOST ENTERTAINING PREDICTION

Women Will Rule the World

Futurist Buckminster Fuller predicted women would rule the world by the 21st century.

In a 1968 *McCall's*, Fuller said: "By the twenty-first century she will have taken over full management of spaceship Earth ... Women will be the undisputed managers of our 60,000-miles-an-hour speeding spaceship Earth in our ever vaster exploration of the universe."

No Professional Sports

Novelist Edward Bellamy imagined no professional sports in the 21st century.

In his 1887 novel, *Looking Backward, 2000-1887* —in which he imagined a socialist paradise existing at the beginning of the third millennium—sports contests are between amateurs only, usually representatives of trade guilds, and not for "money prizes" but "for glory only."

The average NBA salary, at the time of this writing, is about $2.2 million per year.

THE 17ᵀᴴ MOST ENTERTAINING PREDICTION

Somebody Forgot to Tell My Boss

Robert O'Brien predicted the employee of the 21st century would have it pretty good.

In a 1962 *Reader's Digest* article, entitled "Forty Years From Now," he said: "If the trend toward shorter working hours continues, the average worker will put in a 28-hour week. He'll take three-day weekends, four-week vacations with pay. Machines will maintain the nation's productivity."

THE 16TH MOST ENTERTAINING PREDICTION

Bathing Bubble

The book *Golf in the Year 2000*, published in London in 1892, predicted that the 21st century bather would step into "a huge glass globe half full of water," which would then "fly round about and backwards and forwards" until the bather was clean.

THE 15TH MOST ENTERTAINING PREDICTION

Just Two More Popes

Pope John Paul II will be followed by just two more popes, according to a medieval legend.

St. Malachy was an Irish archbishop who lived from 1094-1148. He was on his way to visit the pope when he supposedly had a vision of all the popes from his day till the end of the world. According to the legend, the vision was tucked away in church archives until 1595, when its discovery caused a stir—because the description of popes from Malachy's time until 1595 seemed so accurate.

What does this have to do with just two more popes following John Paul II? Malachy's list had 112 popes. John Paul II is the 110th pope since Malachy's day. (By the way, the last Pope—the one following John Paul's successor—is supposed to be called Peter.)

We'll have wait and see about this prediction, but don't hold your breath. As the writers of *The Millennium Book* point out, "Malachy's descriptions of the future popes sound accurate only for the period between the alleged vision and the 'rediscovery' of the list in 1595."

THE 14TH MOST ENTERTAINING PREDICTION

God Coming to Garland, Texas

Transplanted Taiwanese cult leader Hon-Ming Chen predicted God would come to Garland, Texas, in 1998.

On December 23, 1997, Chen—a former sociology professor, who also declared that he fathered Jesus Christ 2,500 years ago—held a news conference and predicted: "Next year, that is in 1998, on March 31 exactly at 10 a.m., God will change into human being and step on Earth exactly at this place."

Chen said God would arrive in Garland on the "Godplane" (along with other aircraft that had been lost in other dimensions), would (conveniently) take on Chen's form, and save the West from nuclear annihilation in 1999.

Other events Chen predicted would happen before 2000: Noah's Ark found during floods in east Asia, 40 days of rain in Taiwan, and Taiwan's nuclear power plants igniting and killing most of its inhabitants.

THE 13TH MOST ENTERTAINING PREDICTION

Touched by an Alien

Astrologer Noel Tyl predicted the United States would make contact with "intelligence from outer space."

In his 1996 book, *Predictions For A New Millennium*, Tyl predicted: "As early as 2004, possibly in the late Summer, the United States could well be in first contact with intelligence from outer space ... A superior intelligence will have chosen to touch the earth."

THE 12TH MOST ENTERTAINING PREDICTION

Nostradamus Predicts Catastrophe in 1999

Famous 16th century predictor Michel Nostradamus, in a prediction in which he uncharacteristically names a date, forecast the advent of a "King of Terror" in June, 1999:

"In the year 1999 and seven months,

"from the sky will come the great King of Terror.

"He will bring back to life the great King of the Angolmois.

"Before and after, Mars reigns happily."

-*Centuries*, 10.72.

"Mars" is the god of war in Roman mythology. The "King of Terror" has been interpreted as the antichrist, a meteor, a nuclear bomb, etc. The "Angolmois" have been interpreted as invading Chinese.

Nostradamus is difficult to translate and interpret because he wrote, as the authors of *The Millennium Book* point out, "in a bewildering combination of ancient and medieval languages." His famous work *Centuries* is a collection of about 950 quatrains (four-line poems) arranged in groups of one hundred, thus the title *Centuries*.

Nostradamus is also difficult to understand because of his abundant use of symbolic language, and because the poems aren't in chronological order: a poem that supposedly predicted the death of France's Henry II in 1559 follows predictions that supposedly foretold Napoleon's rise and the assassination of John Kennedy.

Nostradamus (his real name was Michel de Nostredame) was born in France in 1502. His family converted from Judaism to Catholicism by the time he was nine. He trained as a doctor, but experienced a personal and professional tragedy when his wife and children died of the plague. He then married a wealthy widow and settled in Salon and had his visions.

The following prediction paved the way for his fame:

"The young lion will overcome the older one,

"In a field of combat in single fight:

"He will pierce his eyes in the golden cage:

"Two wounds in one, then he dies a cruel death."

-*Centuries*, 1.35.

Four years later France's Henry II died following a friendly joust with a younger man. Henry was injured when the young man's lance splintered on contact with Henry's and penetrated Henry's gilt helmet ("the golden cage"), piercing his eye. Another splinter from the shaft is said to have pierced Henry's throat ("Two wounds in one"). Ten days later Henry died of the wounds.

Word of this prediction caused a stir (some say the poem has been re-translated to sound more accurate than it actually was). Among those impressed was Henry's widow, Catherine de Medici, and her support helped Nostradamus gain his fame. He died in 1566 at the age of 62.

THE 11TH MOST ENTERTAINING PREDICTION

The End of Democracy

H.G. Wells (*The Time Machine*, *The War of the Worlds*) predicted democracy would not last.

In his 1901 series in *The North American Review* about "the way things will probably go in this new century," Wells expressed his belief that democracy was merely a popular fiction propped up by political bosses and other elite, which would eventually lead to war (since elected officials gained and maintained their positions by arousing patriotic fever), which would in turn lead to the end of democracy (since war was impossible for a democracy to effectively execute). Power would then fall into "the hands of a new class of intelligent and scientifically educated men."

THE 10TH MOST ENTERTAINING PREDICTION

Underwear Converted into Candy

Waldemar Kaempffert, Science Editor of the *New York Times*, predicted that by the 21st century we might be eating our own—or someone else's!—underwear.

In his 1950 *Popular Mechanics* article, entitled "Miracles You'll See In The Next Fifty Years," Kaempffert said "a vast amount of research" would enable us to supplement our food supply in some unexpected ways: "Thus sawdust and wood pulp are converted into sugary foods. Discarded paper table 'linen' and rayon underwear are bought by chemical factories to be converted into candy."

THE 9TH MOST ENTERTAINING PREDICTION

Silicone Injections in Every Make-up Kit

Science fiction writer Frederik Pohl predicted silicone injections in every girl's make-up kit.

According to a 1967 *New York Times Magazine* article, "They Live In The Year 2000," Pohl addressed a "management-planning session" of Dow Corning Corporation and said: "Silicone injection apparatus is going to be as common in a girl's make-up kit as the eyebrow pencil and lipstick are today," and added with a smile, "You take it from there."

THE 8TH MOST ENTERTAINING PREDICTION

A Cure for Grouchy Spouses

A 1966 *Time* article predicted that "drug control of personality will be widely accepted well before the year 2000."

For example, "If a wife or husband seems to be unusually grouchy on a given evening ... a spouse will be able to pop down to the corner drugstore, buy some anti-grouch pills, and slip them into the coffee."

"Or," said the article, "a lackadaisical person could be dosed into a sense of ambition."

THE 7ᵀᴴ MOST ENTERTAINING PREDICTION

Your Brain Wired to a Computer

A *U.S. News & World Report* article said it was "within the realm of possibility by the year 2000" that mental capacity would by improved "by connecting one's brain directly with a computer."

The article, reporting the findings of the Hudson Institute, appeared in 1967.

THE 6TH MOST ENTERTAINING PREDICTION

A Helicopter in Your Backpack

A 1962 *Science News Letter* article, citing Westinghouse's consumer products vice president Chris J. Witting, predicted that between the year 2000 and the year 2050 citizens would begin to carry their own personal helicopters on their backs.

Said the article: "If a man feels like taking off, he can literally take off. He can carry his own light-weight helicopter, with collapsible blades, in a small, neat case on his back."

Sounds cool!

THE 5TH MOST ENTERTAINING PREDICTION

"We Deliver!"

John Elfreth Watkins, Jr., predicted the home delivery service of restaurants, but it turned out somewhat different than he imagined.

In his December 1900 *Ladies' Home Journal* article, entitled "What May Happen In The Next Hundred Years," Watkins said: "Ready-cooked meals will be ... served hot or cold to private houses in pneumatic tubes or automobile wagons. The meal being over, the dishes used will be packed and returned to the cooking establishments where they will be washed."

Good thing the "pneumatic tubes" part of Watkins' prediction didn't come true—the thought of a Domino's pizza flying toward your home might be a little scary.

THE 4TH MOST ENTERTAINING PREDICTION

An "Airship" with Bat-like Wings

Novelist Paul Devinne predicted that the "airship"—that is, the plane—of the 21st century would have "two tremendous bat-like wings ... vibrating gently, as if impatient to begin their aërial flight."

Devinne made the prediction in his 1902 novel *The Day of Prosperity*. His plane would fly by means of an antigravity device. "Thus the vessel, instead of being attracted by the earth, may be repelled by it; that is to say, may have a tendency to ascend instead of descend."

THE 3RD MOST ENTERTAINING PREDICTION

Eve Takes Off Her Leaf

Futurist Buckminster Fuller predicted a Garden of Eden look for women in the 21st century.

In a 1968 *McCall's* article, entitled "Why Women Will Rule The World," he said: "The tendency to expose the female body will continue to ever greater degree, until woman regains her Garden of Eden freedom and grace." The reason? "Progressive nakedness, contrary to puritanical thinking, progressively lessens the curiosity of the male and slows the baby-production rate. It was not until Eve put on her leaf that baby-making started."

Fuller said: "While women may be completely naked or only fig-leafed during some hours, at other times they will put on extravagant costumes," or "uniforms"—when they want to be taken seriously in the business world.

THE 2ND MOST ENTERTAINING PREDICTION

Doctors Refund Fees If Patient Not Cured

Novelist Samuel Madden predicted that doctors would refund their fees if they failed to cure the patient.

Samuel Madden made this prediction in 1733 in his book, *Memoirs of the Twentieth Century*, one of the first futuristic novels ever written. In the novel a citizen of 1997 states: "Another method they introduc'd here, and which produc'd a great care in the physician of his patient's recovery, was, obliging the Doctor to refund half his fees in case of the death of the sick person." This new custom "spurr'd on all practitioners to do their utmost to serve their patients, or to pay a reasonable fine for their want of success."

THE #1 MOST ENTERTAINING PREDICTION

Golf the Chief Pursuit of Man

The book *Golf in the Year 2000* depicts golf as the chief pursuit of the male population in the 21st century, leaving "trivial matters, such as Church and State, financial establishments, and so on" to women.

The book, which was published in London in 1892, is about a citizen of 1892 who falls into a trance and awakens in the year 2000. He finds some remarkable changes have been made to the game of golf: clubs that record their own score, a mechanical "caddie" that follows the golfer around the course by means of a magnet, golfing jackets that shout "fore," prize money at stake in every round—and golf matches that settle disputes between nations the way war used to.

One thing about golf in the 21st century hasn't changed, however: the "same old excuses."

ENDNOTES

100. Waldemar Kaempffert, "Miracles You'll See In The Next Fifty Years," *Popular Mechanics,* February 1950, pp. 270, 272.

99. Gail Collins and Dan Collins, *The Millennium Book,* A Dolphin Book published by Doubleday, 1991, pp. 118-9.

98. "Fashion & Fantasy," *McCall's,* March 1968, p. 93.

97. William H. Honan, "They Live In The Year 2000," *New York Times Magazine,* April 9, 1967, p. 56.

96. Samuel Madden, *Memoirs of the Twentieth Century, Being Original Letters of State under George the Sixth,* in the Foundation of the Novel series, Garland Publishing, 1972, p. 344.

95. Jeane Dixon, *Jeane Dixon, My Life and Prophecies. Her own story as told to Rene Noorbergen,* William Morrow and Company, 1969, pp. 156-7.

94. Henry Paradyne, "The World in 2009," *Harper's Weekly,* April 3, 1909, p. 25.

93.   Winston Churchill, "Fifty Years Hence," *Popular Mechanics,* March 1932, p. 395.

92. Joe Fisher with Peter Commins, *Predictions,* Van Nostrand Reinhold Company, 1980, p. 56.

91. Joe Fisher with Peter Commins, *Predictions,* Van Nostrand Reinhold Company, 1980, p. 106.

90. Jeane Dixon, *Jeane Dixon, My Life and Prophecies. Her own story as told to Rene Noorbergen,* William Morrow and Company, 1969, p. 151.

89. Robert O'Brien, "Forty Years From Now," *Reader's Digest,* February 1962, p. 50.

88. *The People's Almanac Presents The Book of Predictions,* William Morrow and Company, 1980, p. 279.

87. "Home, Sweet Home of the Future," *Popular Mechanics,* June 1928, pp. 923-7.

86. "The Futurists: Looking Toward A.D. 2000," *Time,* February 25, 1966, p. 28.

85. *Kiplinger forecasts: The New American Boom,* Kiplinger Washington Editors, 1986, p. 140.

84. Betty Cuniberti, "Far-Outlook Bathroom Partying Tops Future Shocks," *The Arizona Republic,* January 1, 1987,   p. F1.

83. David Goodman Croly, *Glimpses of the Future: Suggestions as to the Drift of Things,* G.P. Putnam's Sons, 1888, pp. 171-3.

82. H.G. Wells, "Anticipations: An Experiment in Prophecy," *The North American Review,* September 1901, pp. 72-3.

81. R.G. Ruste, *American Heritage Prognosis A.D. 2000,* Exposition Press, 1967, p. 18.

80. R.G. Ruste, *American Heritage Prognosis A.D. 2000,* Exposition Press, 1967, p. 20.

79. Jeane Dixon, *Jeane Dixon, My Life and Prophecies. Her own story as told to Rene Noorbergen,* William Morrow and Company, 1969, pp. 153-4.

78. Joe Fisher with Peter Commins, *Predictions,* Van Nostrand Reinhold Company, 1980, p. 123.

77. "The Wondrous World of 1990," *U.S. News & World Report,* January 30, 1967, p. 66.

76. J.A.C.K. (MacCulloch), *Golf in the Year 2000,* T. Fisher Unwin (London), 1892, p. 92.

75. *The People's Almanac Presents The Book of Predictions,* William Morrow and Company, 1980, p. 280.

74. "Menu for the Year 2000," *McCall's,* March 1968, p. 139.

73. Winston Churchill, "Fifty Years Hence," *Popular Mechanics,* March 1932, p. 397.

72. David Goodman Croly, *Glimpses of the Future: Suggestions as to the Drift of Things,* G.P. Putnam's Sons, 1888, pp. 156-160.

71. "Predictions for 1998," *National Examiner,* December 16, 1997, p. 23.

70. "Predictions for 1998," *National Examiner,* December 16, 1997, p. 22.

69. *Time,* February 25, 1966, pp. 28-9.

68. *The People's Almanac Presents The Book of Predictions,* William Morrow and Company, 1980, p. 289.

67. Walter Cronkite, "The Twenty-First Century: The World You'll Live In," *Popular Science Monthly,* April 1967, pp. 100-1.

66. Wesley S. Griswold, "What'll It Be Like in 2000 A.D.?" *Popular Science Monthly,* April 1962, p. 87.

65. Edward Bellamy, *Looking Backward, 2000-1887,* Ticknor and Company, 1887, in the Modern Library edition, Random House, 1951, pp. 94-5.

64. H.G. Wells, "Anticipations: An Experiment in Prophecy," *The North American Review,* September 1901, p. 58.

63. John Elfreth Watkins, Jr., "What May Happen In The Next Hundred Years," *Ladies' Home Journal,* December 1900, p. 8.

62. "Happy Home Life, Year 2000," *Science News Letter,* May 19, 1962, p. 314.

61. Waldemar Kaempffert, "Miracles You'll See In The Next Fifty Years," *Popular Mechanics,* February 1950, p. 116.

60. David Goodman Croly, *Glimpses of the Future: Suggestions as to the Drift of Things,* G.P. Putnam's Sons, 1888, p. 24.

59. "The Futurists: Looking Toward A.D. 2000," *Time,* February 25, 1966, pp. 28-9.

58. Paul Devinne, *The Day of Prosperity: A Vision of the Century to Come,* G.W. Dillingham Company, 1902. Reprinted by Arno Press & The New York Times, 1971, p. 92.

57. Edward Bellamy, *Looking Backward, 2000-1887,* Ticknor and Company, 1887, in the Modern Library edition, Random House, 1951, pp. 121-2.

56. "This is Living in 2000 ...," *Newsweek,* September 28, 1959, p. 49.

55. "The Next 25 Years," *Look,* Jan. 16, 1962, p. 19.

54. "The Next 25 Years," *Look,* Jan. 16, 1962, p. 20.

53. Joe Fisher with Peter Commins, *Predictions,* Van Nostrand Reinhold Company, 1980, p. 149.

52. Robert O'Brien, "Forty Years From Now," *Reader's Digest,* February 1962, p. 51.

51. "The Futurists: Looking Toward A.D. 2000," *Time,* February 25, 1966, pp. 28-9.

50. David Goodman Croly, *Glimpses of the Future: Suggestions as to the Drift of Things,* G.P. Putnam's Sons, 1888, pp. 30, 37.

49. Winston Churchill, "Fifty Years Hence," *Popular Mechanics,* March 1932, p. 397.

48. *Kiplinger forecasts: The New American Boom,* Kiplinger Washington Editors, 1986, p. 143.

47. Edward Bellamy, *Looking Backward, 2000-1887,* Ticknor and Company, 1887, in the Modern Library edition, Random House, 1951, pp. 219-20.

46. Paul Devinne, *The Day of Prosperity: A Vision of the Century to Come,* G.W. Dillingham Company, 1902. Reprinted by Arno Press & The New York Times, 1971, p. 102.

45. J.A.C.K. (MacCulloch), *Golf in the Year 2000,* T. Fisher Unwin (London), 1892, pp. 43-6, 75-8.

44. Waldemar Kaempffert, "Miracles You'll See In The Next Fifty Years," *Popular Mechanics,* February 1950, p. 115.

43. "Fashion & Fantasy," *McCall's,* March 1968, p. 96.

42. Joe Fisher with Peter Commins, *Predictions,* Van Nostrand Reinhold Company, 1980, p. 104.

41. Samuel Madden, *Memoirs of the Twentieth Century, Being Original Letters of State under George the Sixth,* in the Foundation of the Novel series, Garland Publishing, 1972, pp. 331-2.

40. *The People's Almanac Presents The Book of Predictions,* William Morrow and Company, 1980, p. 258.

39. *The People's Almanac Presents The Book of Predictions,* William Morrow and Company, 1980, p. 282.

38. *The People's Almanac Presents The Book of Predictions,* William Morrow and Company, 1980, p. 282.

37. "Life in the Year 2001," *McCall's*, March 1968, p. 85.

36. H.G. Wells, "Anticipations: An Experiment in Prophecy," *The North American Review,* September 1901, p. 57.

35. Joe Fisher with Peter Commins, *Predictions,* Van Nostrand Reinhold Company, 1980, p. 102.

34. *The People's Almanac Presents The Book of Predictions,* William Morrow and Company, 1980, p. 28.

33. "Predictions for 1998," *National Examiner,* December 16, 1997, p. 23.

32. "Predictions for 1998," *National Examiner,* December 16, 1997, p. 23.

31. *The People's Almanac Presents The Book of Predictions,* William Morrow and Company, 1980, p. 329.

30. "The Futurists: Looking Toward A.D. 2000," *Time,* February 25, 1966, p. 28.

29. "Happy Home Life, Year 2000," *Science News Letter,* May 19, 1962, p. 314.

28. Waldemar Kaempffert, "Miracles You'll See In The Next Fifty Years," *Popular Mechanics,* February 1950, p. 266.

27. Wesley S. Griswold, "What'll It Be Like in 2000 A.D.?" *Popular Science Monthly,* April 1962, p. 84.

26. *The People's Almanac Presents The Book of Predictions,* William Morrow and Company, 1980, p. 28.

25. *Kiplinger forecasts: The New American Boom,* Kiplinger Washington Editors, 1986, pp. 148-9.

24. *The People's Almanac Presents The Book of Predictions,* William Morrow and Company, 1980, p. 256.

23 Jeane Dixon, *Jeane Dixon, My Life and Prophecies. Her own story as told to Rene Noorbergen,* William Morrow and Company, 1969, p. 141.

22. Noel Tyl, *Predictions For A New Millennium,* Llewellyn Publications, 1996, pp. 127-8.

21. Waldemar Kaempffert, "Miracles You'll See In The Next Fifty Years," *Popular Mechanics,* February 1950, p. 264.

20. Noel Tyl, *Predictions For A New Millennium,* Llewellyn Publications, 1996, pp. 222-3.

19. Buckminster Fuller, "Why Women Will Rule The World," *McCall's,* March 1968, pp. 10-11.

18. Edward Bellamy, *Looking Backward, 2000-1887,* Ticknor and Company, 1887, in the Modern Library edition, Random House, 1951, p. 160.

17. Robert O'Brien, "Forty Years From Now," *Reader's Digest,* February 1962, p. 49.

16. J.A.C.K. (MacCulloch), *Golf in the Year 2000,* T. Fisher Unwin (London), 1892, pp. 16-7.

15. Gail Collins and Dan Collins, *The Millennium Book,* A Dolphin Book published by Doubleday, 1991, p. 105.

14. James Pinkerton, "God due in Texas in March 1998, sect's leader says," *The Arizona Republic,* December 26, 1997.

13. Noel Tyl, *Predictions For A New Millennium,* Llewellyn Publications, 1996, p. 259.

12. Gail Collins and Dan Collins, *The Millennium Book,* A Dolphin Book published by Doubleday, 1991, pp. 98-9, 102.

11. H.G. Wells, "Anticipations: An Experiment in Prophecy," *The North American Review,* September 1901, pp. 263-79.

10. Waldemar Kaempffert, "Miracles You'll See In The Next Fifty Years," *Popular Mechanics,* February 1950, pp. 116-7.

9. William H. Honan,"They Live In The Year 2000," *New York Times Magazine,* April 9, 1967, pp. 57, 59.

8. "The Futurists: Looking Toward A.D. 2000," *Time,* February 25, 1966, p. 29.

---

7. "In Your Future: Robot 'Slaves,' Instant Knowledge, Sea Farms ...," *U.S. News & World Report,* April 10, 1967, p. 113.

6. "Happy Home Life, Year 2000," *Science News Letter,* May 19, 1962, p. 314.

5. John Elfreth Watkins, Jr., "What May Happen In The Next Hundred Years," *Ladies' Home Journal,* December 1900, p. 8.

4. Paul Devinne, *The Day of Prosperity: A Vision of the Century to Come,* G.W. Dillingham Company, 1902. Reprinted by Arno Press & The New York Times, 1971, pp. 195-196.

3. Buckminster Fuller, "Why Women Will Rule The World," *McCall's,* March 1968, pp. 10-11.

2. Samuel Madden, *Memoirs of the Twentieth Century, Being Original Letters of State under George the Sixth,* in the Foundation of the Novel series, Garland Publishing, 1972, pp. 342-3.

1. J.A.C.K. (MacCulloch), *Golf in the Year 2000*, T. Fisher Unwin (London), 1892

ABOUT THE AUTHORS

William and Lynette Ray have been married for over thirty years. They are both graduates of Grand Canyon University, and William holds the Master of Divinity degree from Southwestern Baptist Theological Seminary.

William is also the author of *Answered Prayer: The Jesus Plan, Bible Sidekick: Study Helps for Believers New and Old,* and the novel *Burden Stone.*